A RARE THING . . .
TO PUT IT MILDLY . . .

John Gunther says of Gamal Abdel Nasser that it is a rare thing, to put it mildly, for the president of a country to confess "that he had been the leader of a murder squad."

Here is Nasser's own account in this book:

We, the whole generation, began to move toward violence. I confess, and I hope the Attorney-General will not incriminate me on account of this confession, that political assassinations blazed in my inflamed mind . . . I thought of assassinating many whom I regarded as obstacles between our country and its future . . . Our life was like an exciting detective story. We had great secrets; we had symbols; we hid in the darkness and arranged our pistols and bombs side by side . . .

I remember one night in particular . . . We had prepared everything necessary for action. We selected one to put out of the way . . . The plot was to shoot him as he returned home at night.

The appointed night came and I went out myself with the squad of execution. Everything went as we imagined. The person came and bullets were fired at him. The squad of execution withdrew . . . I started my motor car and dashed away . . .

I got home, threw myself on the bed, my mind in a fever, my heart and conscience incessantly boiling. The cries, moans and wails and the appeals for help still rang in my ears . . . Suddenly I found myself exclaiming, "I wish he would not die." I rushed anxiously to the morning papers. I was happy to find that the individual whose assassination I plotted was destined to live.

THE PHILOSOPHY OF THE REVOLUTION

U. N. Secretary-General Hammarskjold and President Nasser

GAMAL ABDEL
NASSER

THE
PHILOSOPHY
OF THE
REVOLUTION

WITH AN INTRODUCTION BY
JOHN S. BADEAU

AND BIOGRAPHICAL SKETCH BY
JOHN GUNTHER

ECONOMICA BOOKS

Smith, Keynes & Marshall, Publishers

4498 Main Street, Buffalo 26

ECONOMICA BOOKS

on

ECONOMICS, POLITICS AND BUSINESS

Titles published or in preparation

PROSPERITY WITHOUT INFLATION   *by* Arthur F. Burns
THE MEANS TO PROSPERITY   *by* S. H. Slichter, J. M. Keynes, et al.
THE WEALTH OF NATIONS (Selected Chapters)   *by* Adam Smith
SELECTIONS IN ECONOMICS   *by* A. D. Butler and R. C. Epstein
INVENTORS AND MONEY MAKERS   *by* F. W. Taussig
THE RUBLE WAR   *by* Howard K. Smith, et al.
THE UNITED NATIONS   *by* Benjamin Cohen
MAKING MONEY IN TODAY'S MARKET   *by* Ralph C. Epstein
THE GREAT GAME OF POLITICS   *by* Frank R. Kent

TABLE OF CONTENTS

Editor's Note 11

Introduction, by John S. Badeau 13

Part I 25

Part II 43

Part III 57

Appendix

Biographical Note, by John Gunther . . 81

Two Views of Nasser:

(1) *What is Nasser Like?* by Richard
D. Robinson 91

(2) *Arab Nationalism and Nasser,*
by George Kirk 97

EDITOR'S NOTE

This volume is the result of a careful study by *Economica Books* of several available versions of Nasser's essay. The translation used is one published by Dar Al-Maaref in Egypt, and given by President Nasser in Cairo to the Editor.

Although in spots this translation is stylistically awkward from the standpoint of English readers, its deficiencies do not distort Nasser's meaning. Another version (for example, Nolte's mentioned below) would offer American readers a far smoother English style, but would necessarily lack something of the original — albeit naive — vigor of the more literal translation here printed. Accordingly, the text of the Dar Al-Maaref translation has been preserved excepting for the correction of certain errors in spelling or grammar. It has, however, been abridged by approximately 20 per cent.

In this condensation, the omissions are either of repetitive or rambling passages, or of occasional passages on medieval Egyptian history. Nothing controversial has been omitted, nor any remarks bearing on Nasser's attitude toward Israel.

The notes are by Richard H. Nolte of The Rockefeller Foundation, whose own annotated translation appeared as an Institute of Current World Affairs Newsletter and as an American Universities Field Staff Report early in 1954.

The introduction by Dr. Badeau is based on the Dar Al-Maaref translation and is prepared especially for *Economica Books*. We are most fortunate in having persuaded Dr. Badeau to write it on short notice just prior to his departure for Africa. As former president of the American University in Cairo, and now as president of the Near East Foundation, he has had long and extensive knowledge of Egypt's conditions, on which he is an acknowledged authority. His penetrating introduction to *The Philosophy* reflects both this broad background and a refreshing absence of bias with regard to a man who is surely one of the most controversial and important persons in the world today.

INTRODUCTION

By John S. Badeau[1]

The day after the army coup d'etat in Egypt (July 23, 1952) General Mohammed Neguib, leader of the Free Officers, cabled a friend in England, "How's that!"

The revolutionary government of Egypt has had ample occasion to repeat these exultant words many times in the following seven years. A series of bold *fait accomplis* has successfully challenged the West; Egypt has rapidly emerged as the dominant influence in the Arab world, and its revolution has spilled over the Nile Valley to become the "wave of the future" in adjacent lands.

What are the meaning and secret of this movement? Is it indeed the spontaneous combustion of long smoldering social discontent — or only its clever utilization by a new group of leaders? And what of Gamal Abdel Nasser, its symbol and center? Estimates of him run from the Arab acclamation of a new Saladin to bitter Western diatribes against an irresponsible dictator, delivering himself and his people into Soviet hands.

[1]President, Near East Foundation.

13

In studying the Egyptian revolution, only two documents from Nasser himself are available to Western readers. One is an article appearing in the quarterly journal, *Foreign Affairs,* of January, 1955; the other is *The Philosophy of the Revolution,* here reissued in translation. Both ought to be read as preludes to any serious estimates of Nasser and the Revolution.

The Philosophy of the Revolution was first published in Cairo in 1953 as a modest pamphlet. It was third in an informational series sponsored by the Revolutionary Council under the general title, "We Have Chosen For You." There is some question as to whether it was a completely new work, or whether it was composed by skillfully blending excerpts from speeches with personal notes. It did not attract major attention at the time, nor was it widely distributed in the Arab world.

With the Suez Canal crisis, Nasser suddenly filled the Middle Eastern horizon, becoming both a regional hero and a vexing international problem. To restless and frustrated Arab nationalists, he indeed seemed a second Saladin, turning the tables on Western "imperialism." To the West, he appeared as the ominous and lengthening shadow of xenophobic nationalism, dangerously allied with Soviet ambition in one of the world's most strategic areas.

Almost overnight *The Philosophy* became a source book on "Nasserism." It went through five editions in Arabic, was widely distributed by Egyptian informational offices and appeared in shortened or serial form in the Middle East press. Western writers seized on *The Philosophy* as documentation for their estimates of Nasser's character and plans. Excerpts (frequently quoted out of context) appeared in political columns and no less a person than the Premier of France declared it to be another *Mein Kampf,* outlining the sinister policies of a new Hitler. The account of Nasser's conspiratorial school days was cited as revealing an inherently violent character and the section on "A Role in Search of a Hero" was declared proof of a dictatorial power complex.

This estimate of *The Philosophy* was due mainly to Suez hysteria and can only be held by those who have failed to read it carefully. The book is not a systematic and closely reasoned account of either the political philosophy or future plans of Nasser and his revolutionary associates. One Cairo story has it that the substance of the manuscript came from off-the-record thoughts of Nasser, jotted down at home and saved from the children and the wastebasket by his wife. The tale may be apocryphal, but (like so many bazaar rumors) its substance is true. "Philosophy" is too ambitious a title for the result — as Nasser himself admits in the opening paragraph. At best the book is a collection of "reflections" or "musings" on the early experiences of a revolutionary who did not know quite where he was going but was anxious to be on his way.

That *The Philosophy* is not a detailed forecasting of political policies is made clear by subsequent events. Some of Nasser's major coups — the arms purchase from Czechoslovakia, the nationalization of the Suez Canal, the union with Syria — are not mentioned. Especially noticeable is the absence of any emphasis on the role of Nasser as the hero and Egypt as the leader of a united Arab world, as the restorers of an Arab Empire. The "Arab Circle" is indeed mentioned in the oft-quoted passage on the three spheres of Egyptian destiny, but without any indication that Egypt intends to lose her identity in the nebulous "Arab nation" that is the current theme of so much Arab nationalism. Nasser speaks of Egypt as lying "close to the Arab world whose life is intermingled with ours" and whose "history merges with ours" — but at this stage he is still first an Egyptian and not an Arab, least of all a leader planning to bring the entire Arab world under his control.

One reason why later political developments are not forecast in *The Philosophy* is because the Egyptian revolution has been largely pragmatic in character. As *The Philosophy* frankly states, the Free Officers started out without any very clear idea as to where they were going. Nasser likens them to an "advance vanguard" storming the "walls of the fort of tyranny." But once the fort had fallen and the unlamented King had taken his unlamented farewell, there was no clear plan of action. Subsequent revolutionary policy — both internal and external — developed in response to immediate situations on a pragmatic basis, rather than as parts of any master plan. The nationalization of the Suez Canal was precipitated by America's cancelling of its High Dam offer, and was a counter-attack to regain prestige as well as a financial measure to shore up the Egyptian economy. The creation of the United Arab Republic, while resting upon desultory Syrian-Egyptian cooperation, was brought about because of sudden political developments in Syria rather than as a carefully planned Egyptian maneuver.

17

But if *The Philosophy of the Revolution* is neither a philosophy nor a *Mein Kampf,* what is it?

First, it is a source document for the origins of the Egyptian revolution. In his "Egypt's Destiny", Mohammed Neguib has given a more detailed account of the events that led up to the coup d'etat, but Nasser expresses more adequately the psychology of the revolution, the frustration and hope out of which it was born. His account makes it clear that the coup was not due simply to a power hungry military clique who saw an opportunity to turn out the King. A winter of popular discontent had been steadily settling over the country ever since the Palestine war — as those of us who lived in Egypt fully knew. It is not strange if the spring of revolution was not far behind. How far the present government of Egypt rests upon and retains its early idealistic character is a matter of debate; but Nasser's picture of its origin is accurate.

That picture is significant for what it does not include as well as for what it does. There is no bitter diatribe against Israel, and there is no dedication to wipe out Israel. Nasser specifically repudiates the idea that the Palestine War was the real cause of the revolution. By his own account, the Palestine experience did two things to him; it taught the value of an underground movement (which he discussed with an Israeli officer) and it convinced him that the basic problem everywhere was "Imperialism." In *The Philosophy,* Israel is viewed primarily as a facet of British imperial policy and Nasser's resentment at this stage was focused on the British rather than on the Israelis. This was to change with later events.

A second value of *The Philosophy* is as a bench mark for the study of Nasser's character. In these early thoughts, he appears as a devoted, sincere and somewhat confused young nationalist, typical of the frustration and idealism of his generation. When he writes that "the revolution first started within us as individuals, in ourselves as normal types of the youth of our generation," he is correct. I have known many young Nassers among my student friends in Cairo. Their schoolboy plots were sometimes dangerous, often pitiable. For them the times were completely out of joint and they sought hope in extremist movements like the Muslim Brotherhood,[1] until the

---

[1]A fanatical religious group that tried to assassinate Nasser in October, 1954. See Gunther's Biographical Sketch in the Appendix. Muslim may be spelled either "Muslim" or "Moslem"; in this book "Muslim" is used.

Revolution came. Then in Nasser and his associates they found a pattern of action that seemed to promise the new Egypt for which they looked. This is one reason why Nasser appeals so strongly to the student group in Arab countries; he is both the symbol and substance of the national regeneration that is their confused concern.

But success may spoil a Nasser as well as a Rock Hunter. The amazing diplomatic triumphs by which Nasser has established his position as the potential leader of the Arab world have had a profound effect on both his policies and objectives. He has become more confident in leadership, more calculating in his appeal to the crowd, more ready to enforce internal control. Widely differing views of his motivation and purposes are held today, even in the Arab world. But the Nasser of *The Philosophy* is where he started.

Yet whatever changes the later years have brought, there are characteristics that bind the Nasser of today quite closely to the Nasser of *The Philosophy*. One is his "capacity for swift action and initiative."

"We make a mistake in the definition of power," he writes, "power is not merely shouting aloud. Power is to act positively."

This conviction is based on two experiences.

One is that, in the past, Egyptian discontent expended itself in mobs, street demonstrations and shouted slogans — the kind of action that led to the burning of Cairo in 1952. The other experience was the "shocking" popular inertia of the first days of the Revolution. After the vanguard had thrown out the King, it waited, thinking that "we would soon be followed by the solid masses marching to goal." But the masses did not march and the professional political leaders and university intellectuals could not propose any constructive plan of action. "Every leader we came to wanted to assassinate his rival" — this was the only program the Revolution found !

Out of these experiences and out of his Army background, ("throughout my life I have had faith in militarism," writes Nasser) has emerged the policy of "swift action" so characteristic of Nasser and his Revolutionary Council. Through it some of his greatest triumphs have been achieved. With a shrewd sense of timing, he has often caught the Western world off balance and presented it with a *fait accompli* instead of protracted diplomatic negotiations.

A second continuing element in Nasser's leadership and program is his conviction that "we are in the throes of two revolutions and not one."

21

The second revolution is "social, in which the classes of society would struggle against each other until justice for all countrymen has been gained." There are those who maintain that the social reforms of the Egyptian Revolution are more grandiose than effective, designed to impress the populace rather than substantially alter their living conditions. Certainly some of Nasser's most dramatic social projects have had this in view, but the genuine social base of the Revolution is not thereby discredited. Notable social progress has been made — especially when measured against the almost insoluble nature of Egypt's economic condition with its severe limitation on arable land and the pressure of population increase.

Approximately half a million acres of land have been distributed to peasants, food production has increased 12 per cent in six years, and a new credit and cooperative system for farmers is somewhat easing their financial problems. Whether this promising beginning can be continued, with the national budget burdened with growing military expenditures and the national economy mortgaged to the Soviet bloc, is doubtful. But that Nasser sincerely feels that "it is imperative that we should proceed with the two revolutions together" cannot seriously be doubted.

It is this identification of political with social revolution that has spread and supported Nasser's influence throughout the Arab world. And it is this identification that poses the West with its most serious diplomatic problem. How can the West at times oppose the growing political influence of revolutionary Egypt without appearing to oppose the badly needed and eagerly sought social revolution that Nasser's leadership represents?

PART I

Before proceeding with this discourse I would like to pause at the word "Philosophy." It looks big and sounds grand.

The truth is the Philosophy of the Revolution of July 23rd[1] should be treated by professors who should search deeply into it for the roots spreading at the very depth of our history. The stories of national struggles have no gaps that can be filled with nonsense. Neither have they the surprises that spring into existence without preludes.

I do not pretend to be a professor of history. This is the last thing my imagination may entertain. Nevertheless, if I were to attempt to study the story of our struggle like a schoolboy I would say, for instance, that the revolution of July 23rd is the realization of a hope that the people of Egypt, in modern times, have aspired to since they began to think of governing themselves and since they decided to be the masters of their fate.

One attempt failed to realize this hope when

[1]On this date in 1952, Colonel Nasser, General Neguib, and their followers in a bloodless revolution, seized the Government of Egypt and on July 26 forced King Farouk off his throne.

25

El Sayyed Omar Makram led the movement for appointing Mohamed Aly[2] viceroy of Egypt in the name of its people. Another attempt failed to fulfil this aspiration when Arabi[3] rose demanding a constitution. Other vain attempts followed during the intellectual fervour in the period between the revolt of Arabi and the Revolution of 1919. This latter was led by Saad Zaghloul[4] who again failed to reach his goal.

It is not true that the revolution of July 23rd started on account of the results of the war in Palestine. Neither was it caused by defective arms, to which officers and men fell victims. It is still further from the truth to attribute it to

[2]Led by the Azharite religious notable, Sheikh Omar Makram, and others, the people of Cairo saw in Mohamed Aly a champion against the tyranny of the Mameluke nobility and proclaimed him governor of Cairo. He became the founder of the dynasty which ended recently with Farouk.

[3]Colonel Arabi led a military revolt in 1881 on behalf of the Egyptian people, demanding a constitution and parliamentary government. At first successful and wildly popular, the revolution was put down by British troops in 1882—the beginning of the British occupation.

[4]Immediately after the First World War, the prominent Egyptian statesman and nationalist, Saad Zaghloul, sought to lead a deputation to England to treat for complete independence. He was refused; and after failing to gain for Egypt's claim the ear of the Peace Conference in Versailles, he returned home to organize the many postwar ideological and economic discontents at large in Egypt into a coherent demand for independence. The British exiled him to Malta, whereupon anti-British violence broke out all over Egypt. British troops only gradually restored order. He was released, and later formed the Wafdist Party.

the crisis of the elections of the Officers' Club.[5] In my opinion its causes are deeper and farther. Had the officers endeavoured to avenge themselves because they were cheated in Palestine or because the defective arms strained their nerves and because they suffered an indignity in the elections of the Officers' Club, the whole affair would not have deserved to be called a revolution. A mere mutiny was the likely description even if it were attributed to causes fair and just in themselves. All these were incidental. Perhaps their greatest influence was that they urged us to march forward along the road to revolution; but without them we were marching just the same.

Today I am trying to recall all the events that passed and, after years have elapsed since we first thought of the revolution, to go back to the first day I discovered the seeds of revolt within me. That day lies farther back in my life than November 1951, which marked the beginning of the crisis of the Officers' Club elections. The organization of the Liberal Officers[6] was then existing

[5]In the Club elections late in 1951, Farouk tried to force the election of Major-General Hussein Sirry Amer as President of the Administrative Council. Implicated in the arms scandal, Amer had nonetheless been put in command of the Frontier Forces, replacing General Neguib. The Club in defiance elected Neguib President.

[6]A secret movement organized in party cells.

and active. I do not exaggerate when I say that the crisis of the Officers' Club elections was caused, more than anything else, by the activities of the Liberal Officers. We were determined to fight then in order to test the strength of our mass formation and real organization.

That day lies again farther back in my life than May 16, 1944, which marked the start of my life in the Palestine War. As I trace the details of our experience in Palestine I feel a strange sensation. We were fighting in Palestine but our dreams were in Egypt. Our bullets were aimed at the enemy lurking in the trenches in front of us, but our hearts were hovering round our distant Mother Country, which was then a prey to the wolves that ravaged it. In Palestine, Liberal Officers' cells were meeting in trenches and posts studying and searching. And it was in Palestine that Salah Salem and Zakaria Mohyy-el-Din came to me after having penetrated the siege of Falouga;[7] there we sat besieged neither knowing what was to become of that siege nor when it would end. We spoke of nothing but our country and how to deliver it. It was in Palestine that

[7]Elements of the Egyptian army were cut off and surrounded in the "Falouga Pocket" by Israeli forces during the Palestine War. A stubborn defense was put up by the encircled Egyptians who held out until liberated by the truce agreement.

Gamal-el-Din Hussein sat beside me one day
and spoke as his eyes wandered and his thoughts
dispersed; "Do you know what Ahmad Abdel
Aziz[8] had told me before he died?" he asked.
"What did he say?" I asked in return. With a
deep tone of voice and still deeper look he said,
"Listen Gamal, Egypt is the field of our supreme
war effort."

It was not only the friends I met in Palestine
who spoke to me of the future of our country, but
the enemy also played his part in reminding us of
our homeland and its difficulties. A few months
ago I read some articles written upon me by a
Jewish officer named Yerdan Cohen. These were
published in the Jewish Observer. In these
articles he related how he met me during the
contacts and discussions of the Armistice. "The
subject that Gamal Abdel Nasser discussed with
me," he stated, "was Israel's struggle against the
English, how we organized our underground resistance in Palestine and how we succeeded in
mobilizing world public opinion behind us against
them."

The day I discovered the seeds of revolt within
me was still further back than February 4, 1942
[when British tanks surrounded Abdin Palace

[8]Egyptian Commando Officer in the Palestine War.

seeking to force a change of government on King Farouk]. I wrote to a friend later saying, "What is to be done now that the catastrophe has befallen us, and after we have accepted it, surrendered to it and taken it submissively and meekly.

"I really believe," I continued, "that Imperialism is playing a one-card game in order to threaten only. If ever it knew that there were Egyptians ready to shed their blood and to meet force by force it would withdraw and recoil like a harlot. This, of course, is the state or habit of Imperialism everywhere."

Was it our duty, as an army, to do what we did on July 23, 1952?

I have just explained how the revolution of July 23rd was the realization of a hope that dangled before the eyes of the people of Egypt since they began, in modern times, to think of governing themselves and having the final word on their destiny. If this be so, and if what took place on July 23rd was only a military mutiny and not a popular revolt, why was the army then, apart from any other forces, destined to carry out this revolution?

Throughout my life I have had faith in militarism. The soldier's sole duty is to die on the frontiers of his country. Why then was our army compelled to act in the capital and not on the frontier?

Once more, let me reiterate that the defeat in Palestine, the defective arms, the crisis of the Officers' Club election were not the real springs from which the current flowed. They may have accelerated the flood but they could never be the original source. Why then did this duty fall upon the army? This question has often occurred to me. It came to me persistently during the stage of hoping, of thinking and of planning before July 23rd. It repeated itself several times during the experimental period after July 23rd. We had different factors to justify action before July 23rd and to explain to us why it was imperative that the army should act. "If the army does not move," we said to ourselves, "who else will?"

I confess that after July 23rd I suffered fits in which I accused myself, my colleagues and the rest of the army of rashness and folly we committed on July 23rd.

Prior to that date I imagined that the whole nation was on tip-toes and prepared for action, that it awaited the advance of the vanguard and the storming of the outside walls for it to pour down in a solid phalanx marching faithfully to the great goal. I thought we were only the pioneers and the commandoes, that we would only be in the front for a few hours, and that we would be soon followed by the solid masses marching to the goal. My imagination often carried me away. I felt I could hear the rattle of their solid, orderly rows as they marched onwards to the main front. My faith was such as to render everything I heard a concrete fact and not a mere vision.

After July 23rd I was shocked by the reality. The vanguard performed its task; it stormed the walls of the fort of tyranny; it forced Farouk to abdicate and stood by expecting the mass formations to arrive at their ultimate object. It waited and waited. Endless crowds showed up, but how different is the reality from the vision! The multitudes that arrived were dispersed followers and contrasted remnants. The holy march towards the great goal was interrupted. A dismal picture, horrible and threatening, then presented itself. I felt my heart charged with sorrow and dripping with bitterness. The mission of the vanguard had not ended. In fact it was just beginning at that very hour. We needed discipline but found chaos behind our lines. We needed unity but found dissensions. We needed action but found nothing but surrender and idleness. It was from this source and no other that the revolution derived its motto.[9]

We did not expect this shock. We went to the men of ideas for counsel and to the men of experience for guidance, but unfortunately we did not find much of either.

Every leader we came to wanted to assassinate his rival. Every idea we found aimed at the destruction of another. If we were to carry out all that we heard, then there would not be one leader left alive. Not one idea would remain intact. We would cease to have a mission save to remain among the smashed bodies and the broken debris lamenting our misfortune and reproaching our ill-fate.

Complaints and petitions poured upon us in thousands. If these did refer to cases worthy of justice, or mentioned oppression that might be redressed, they would be understandable and

[9]Namely, "Unity, Discipline, Work." The great Egyptian thinker and reformer, Sheikh Muhammad 'Abduh (1849-1905) put forward as the basis of his political program the slogan, "Unity, Discipline, Justice." He anticipated the Revolution in other ways, e.g., in his view that the regeneration of Egyptian society could only be carried out by a just dictatorship. Popular representation made no sense without popular conviction to support it. A just dictatorship, by persuasion and force, could unite the community and instill healthy ideas. Fifteen years would be enough to build the necessary foundations for free representative government. But without such a sound authoritarian regime, fifteen centuries would not suffice.

logical. The majority of these were but persistent demands for revenge as if the revolution were meant to be a weapon for revenge and hatred.

If I were asked then what I required most my instant answer would be, "To hear but one Egyptian uttering one word of justice about another, to see but one Egyptian not devoting his time to criticize wilfully the ideas of another, to feel that there was but one Egyptian ready to open his heart for forgiveness, indulgence and loving his brother Egyptians." Personal and persistent selfishness was the rule of the day. The word "I" was on every tongue. It was the magic solution of every difficulty and the effective cure for every malady.

Often did I meet men, referred to in the press as "great men," of various tendencies and colours, from whom I sought the solution of a difficult problem. I could hear nothing from them save the word "I." He and only he was capable of understanding the problems of economics; the rest were but children creeping on all fours. He and only he was the expert statesman and the rest only learning their a & b and had not got to c. After interviewing any of these men I would go back to my colleagues bitterly exclaiming, "How utterly futile . . .! If we were to ask that man about a difficulty in fishing off the Islands of Hawaii his answer would only be 'I'."

I remember I once visited one of our universities and sat with professors endeavoring to profit by the experience of men of learning. Many spoke and spoke at length. Unfortunately not one of them presented a new idea. Every one introduced himself and listed his moral capacities which, in his view, could perform miracles. Every one eyed me as if I were to him more precious that the treasures of earth or the blessings of eternity. I could not help but remark to them all, "Everyone in his place can perform miracles. The primary duty is to put all energy into it and if you, as university professors, ever thought of students and rendered them, as you should, your principal care, you would provide us with a tremendous force wherewith to build up our country. Let every one remain at his post and strive hard at it. Do not look up to us. Circumstances have compelled us to leave our posts to perform a sacred task. We sincerely wish the country has no further use for us save as professional soldiers in the army. There we would have remained."

I did not wish then to set before them the example of the members of the Revolution Council[10] who, before the crisis summoned them for the supreme task, were performing their duties in the army most diligently. I did not wish to tell them that most of the members of the Revolution Council were professors in the Staff-College . . . a clear proof of their distinction as professional soldiers.

Every nation on earth undergoes two revolutions: One is political, in which it recovers its right for self-government from an imposed despot, or an aggressive army occupying its territory without its consent. The second revolution is social, in which the classes of society would struggle against each other until justice for all countrymen has been gained and conditions have become stable.

Other nations have preceded us along the path of human progress and passed through the two revolutions but not simultaneously. Hundreds of years separated the one from the other. In the case of our nation, it is going through the two revolutions together and at the same time, a great experiment putting us to the test.

Political revolution demands, for its success, the unity of all national elements, their fusion

[10]The cabinet of Neguib and Nasser, consisting mainly of Army officers who were Nasser's associates in the Free Officers movement and in the Revolution of July 23, 1952.

and mutual support, as well as self-denial for the sake of the country as a whole.

One of the first signs of social revolution is that values are shaken and creeds are relaxed; fellow-countrymen struggle against each other, individuals and classes. Corruption, suspicion, hatred and selfishness dominate them. Between the anvil and the hammer we now live in two revolutions; one demanding that we should unite together, love one another and strain every nerve to reach our goal; the other forces us, in spite of ourselves, to disperse and give way to hatred, everyone thinking only of himself.

Between the anvil and the hammer the 1919 Revolution was lost and failed to achieve the results which it ought to have realized. The ranks that massed in 1919 to face tyranny were, after a while, occupied only by internal strife. Tyranny became more arbitrary whether it was in the form of the open forces of occupation or their veiled cat's paws, headed by Sultan Fouad and later by his son Farouk. The nation reaped nothing but a crop of self-suspicion, egoism and hatred, between individuals and classes alike. The hopes which the 1919 Revolution was expected to realize faded. The fact that they only faded and did not die out is due to the hopes that our nation always entertained. These hopes were still alive, and the natural resistance engendered by them was preparing for another trial. Such was the state of affairs that prevailed after the 1919 Revolution and which made the army the only force capable of action.

The situation demanded a homogeneous force. Its members should have faith in each other and should have in their hands such elements of material force as to ensure swift and decisive action. Such conditions did not prevail except in the army.

It was not the army, as I mentioned, that determined its role in the events. The opposite is nearer the truth. It was the events and their evolution that determined for the army its role in the mighty struggle for the liberation of the country.

I have realized from the very beginning that our success depended on our complete understanding of the nature of the conditions we live in as related to our national history.

It was imperative that we should proceed with the two revolutions together. The day we marched along the path of political revolution and dethroned Farouk we took a similar step along the path of social revolution by limiting the

Wide World Photos

Gamal Abdel Nasser

King Farouk in exile on the
Riviera

Wide World Photos

General Neguib with King Ibn Saud of Saudi Arabia

ownership of agricultural land.[11] I still believe until today that the revolution of July 23rd should retain its capacity for swift action and initiative in order that it may fulfill the miracle of proceeding with the two revolutions simultaneously, contradictory as our action may appear to be sometimes.

When a friend of mine came to me one day exclaiming, "You asked for unity to face the English and at the same time you permit the Graft Court to proceed with its work."[12] I listened to him with the image of our big crisis in my mind: the crisis of being between two millstones. One revolution demanded that we should stand in one row and forget the past, while another revolution forced us to restore the lost dignity of moral values and not forget the past.

This was not my will; nor was it the will of those who took part in the revolution of July 23rd. It was the will of fate, of the history of our nation and of the stage it is passing through today.

[11]On August 12, 1952, the new government announced its decision "in principle" to limit land ownership to 200 acres. The Agrarian Reform Law of 1952 was passed September 9, embodying the 200-acre rule.

[12]Referring, apparently, to the prosecutions going on against allegedly corrupt members of the *ancien regime* under the "Where Did You Get It?" law.

PART II

PART II

What is it we want to do? And which is the way to it?

There is no doubt we all dream of Egypt free and strong. No Egyptian would ever differ with another about that. As for the way to liberation and strength, that is the most intricate problem in our lives.

I have felt, since consciousness first dawned within me, that positive action is the only way. But what action?

Ever since I was at the head of demonstrations in Al Nahda School,[1] I have clamoured for complete independence; others repeated my cries; but these were in vain.

They were blown away by the winds and became faint echoes that do not move mountains or smash rocks. Later "positive action" meant in my opinion that all leaders of Egypt should unite on one thing. Rebellious cheering crowds passed our leaders' homes one by one demanding, in the name of the youth of Egypt, that they should unite on one thing. It was a tragedy to

[1] The secondary school that Nasser attended.

my faith that the one thing they united on was the Treaty of 1936.[2]

Then came the second World War and the events that preceded it. Both inflamed our youth and spread fire to its innermost feelings. We, the whole generation, began to move towards violence. I confess, and I hope the Attorney-General will not incriminate me on account of this confession, that political assassinations blazed in my inflamed mind during that period as the only positive action from which we could not escape, if we were to save the future of our country.

I thought of assassinating many whom I regarded as obstacles between our country and its future. I began to expose their crimes and set myself as a judge of their actions and of the harm that these brought upon the country; and then I would follow all this by the sentence that should be passed upon them.

I thought of assassinating the ex-King and those of his men who tampered with our sacred traditions. In this I was not alone. When I sat with others our thoughts passed from thinking to

[2]The Treaty was a recognition by Britain and Egypt of the threat posed by the successful Italian invasion of Ethiopia in 1935-36. It gave Britain the right to station 10,000 men and 400 pilots in Canal Zone bases for 20 years, and could be renegotiated after ten.

planning. Many a design did I draw up those days. Many a night did I lie awake preparing the means for the expected positive action.

Our life was, during this period, like an exciting detective story. We had great secrets; we had symbols; we hid in the darkness and arranged our pistols and bombs side by side. This was the hope we dreamt of. We made many attempts in this direction and I still remember, until today, our feelings and emotions as we dashed along the road to its end.

The truth, however, is I did not feel at ease within myself to consider violence as the positive action essential for the salvation of our country's future. I had within me a feeling of distraction which was a mixture of complex and inter-mingled factors: of patriotism, religion, compassion, cruelty, faith, suspicion, knowledge and ignorance.

Slowly and gently did the idea of political assassination which was blazing in my imagination, begin to die out and lose its value within me as the realization of the expected positive action.

I remember one night in particular which was decisive in directing my thoughts and my dreams along that channel. We had prepared everything necessary for action. We selected one, whom we found essential to put out of the way. We studied the circumstances of the life of this individual, and made the plot in detail. This plot was to shoot him as he returned home at night. We organized a squad of assault which would shoot him, another to guard this first and a third to organize the plan of getting away to safety after the plot had been fully carried out.

The appointed night came and I went out myself with the squad of execution. Everything went to plan as we imagined.

The scene was empty, as we had expected. The squads lay in the hiding places fixed for them. The person whom we wanted to get out of the way came and bullets were fired at him. The squad of execution withdrew, covered in its retreat by the guards, and the operation of getting away began. I started my motor car and dashed away from the scene of the positive action we planned. Cries, wailings and moans suddenly rang in my ears. The wailing of a woman, the voice of a scared child and the continuous feverish appeals for help assailed my ears. I was steeped in my rebellious set of emotions as my car rushed me along. I then became conscious of something strange; the sounds I heard were still tearing my ears, as well as the cries, wails and moans and the feverish appeals for help. I was then away from the scene, further than sound could reach. Nevertheless I felt all these beginning to haunt and chase me.

I got home, threw myself on the bed, my mind in a fever, my heart and conscience incessantly boiling. The cries, moans and wails and the appeals for help still rang in my ears. All night long I could not sleep. I lay on my bed in darkness, lighting one cigarette after another, wandering away with my rebellious thoughts which were driven away by the sounds that haunted me. "Was I right?" I asked myself. With conviction I answered, "My motives were patriotic." "Was this an unavoidable means?" I again asked myself. In doubt I replied: "What could we have done otherwise? Is it possible that the future of our country could change by getting rid of this one individual or another? Is not the question far deeper than this?" In bewilderment I would say to myself: "I almost feel that the question is deeper. We dream of the glory of a nation. Which is more important? That some one should pass away who should pass away or that someone should come who should come."

As I mention this I see rays of light gradually filtering through these crowded sensations.

"What is important," I would say to myself, "is that someone should come who should come. We are dreaming of the glory of a nation: A glory that must be built up." As I tossed on my bed in a room full of smoke and charged with emotions, I found myself asking: "And then?" "And what then?", a mysterious voice called out.

With deep conviction this time I again said to myself, "Our method must change. This is not the positive action we should aim at. The roots of the question go more deeply. The problem is more serious and more far-reaching." At this I felt an undiluted relief which was soon dispersed by the cries, moans, wails and appeals whose echoes resounded inside me. Suddenly I found myself exclaiming, "I wish he would not die." I rushed anxiously to the morning papers. I was happy to find that the individual whose assassination I plotted was destined to live.

But this was not the fundamental problem. The principal question is to find out the positive action. Since then we began to think of something more deeply rooted, more serious and more far-reaching. We began to draw the preliminary lines of the vision that was realized in the night of July 23rd, namely a revolution springing from the very heart of the people, charged with its aspirations and pursuing completely the steps it had previously taken along its destined path.

It was easy then, and I still find it easy now, to shed the blood of ten, twenty, or thirty persons in order to strike fear and panic in the hearts of many hesitants, and thus force them to swallow their passions, their hatred, and their whims. But what result could such an action achieve? I used to think that the only way to face a problem was to trace it to its origin and to try to follow the source from which it began.

Fate has so willed that we should be on the crossroads of the world. Often have we been the road which invaders took and a prey to adventurers. In certain circumstances we found it impossible to explain the factors latent in the soul of our nation without due consideration of these circumstances.

In my opinion we cannot overlook the history of Egypt under the Pharaohs or the reaction between the Greek spirit and ours, the Roman invasion, and Muslim conquest and the waves of Arab migrations that followed.

I believe we should pause for a time and examine the circumstances we went through in the Middle Ages; for it is these that got us up to the stage we are in today.

49

If the Crusades were the dawn of a renaissance in Europe they were also the commencement of the dark ages in our country. Our nation has borne the brunt of the Crusades. They left it exhausted, poverty-stricken and destitute.

Often, when I go back to turning the pages of our history, I feel sorrow tearing my soul as I consider the period when a tyrannical feudalism was formed, a feudalism which had no other object save sucking the blood of life out of our veins and sapping from these veins the remnants of any feeling of power and of dignity. It left in the depth of our souls an effect that we have to struggle long to overcome.

European society passed through the stages of its evolution in an orderly manner. It crossed the bridge between the Renaissance at the end of the Middle Ages and the Nineteenth Century step by step. The stages of this evolution systematically succeeded one another.

In our case everything was sudden. European countries eyed us covetously and regarded us as a crossroad to their colonies in the East and the South.

Torrents of ideas and opinions burst upon us which we were, at that stage of our evolution, incapable of assimilating. Our spirits were still in the Thirteenth Century though the symptoms of the Nineteenth and Twentieth Centuries infiltrated in their various aspects. Our minds were trying to catch up the advancing caravan of humanity.

At one time I complained that the people did not know what they wanted. They were not unanimous in their choice of the way to take. I realized later that I demanded the impossible and that I took no account of the circumstances of our society.

We live in a society that has not yet crystallized. It is still boiling over and restless. It has not yet calmed or settled down, so as to continue its gradual evolution parallel with other nations which preceded it along the road.

I believe, without paying any compliment to people's emotions, that our nation has realized a miracle. Any nation, exposed to the same conditions as our country, could be easily lost. It could be swept away by the torrents that fell upon it. But it stood firm in the violent earthquake.

It is true we nearly lost our equilibrium in some circumstances; but generally we did not fall to the ground. As I consider one normal Egyptian family out of the thousands that live in the capital, I find the following: the father, for example, is a turbanned "fellah" from the heart of the country; the mother a lady descended from Turkish stock; the sons of the family are at a school adopting the English system; the daughters the French. All this lies between the Thirteenth century and the outward appearances of the Twentieth.

As I see this I feel within me I can comprehend the bewilderment and the confusion that assail us. Then I say to myself, "This society will crystallize; its component parts will hold together; it will form a homogeneous entity; but this necessitates that we should strain our nerves during the period of transition."

Such are, then, the roots from which sprang our conditions of today. Such are the sources from which our crisis flows. If I add to these social origins the circumstances for which we expelled Farouk and for which we wish to liberate our country from every foreign soldier; if we add all these together, we shall discover the wide sphere in which we labour and which is exposed, from every side, to the winds, to the violent storm that raged in its corners, to flashing lightning and roaring thunder.

Therefore, one may ask, "Which is the way? and what is our role in it?"

The way is that which leads to economic and political freedom.

Many people come to me and exclaim, "You have angered everybody." To which explanation I always reply, "It is not people's anger that influences the situation. The question should be: Was what aroused their anger for the good of the country or for the interest of whom?" I realize we have upset big land-owners; but was it possible not to upset them and yet behold some of us owning thousands of acres, while others do not own the plot of land wherein they are buried after their death?

I realize we have aroused the wrath of old politicians; but was it possible not to do so and yet behold our country a victim to their passions, their corruption and their struggle for the spoils of office?

I realize we have angered many government officials; but without this was it possible to spend more than half the budget on officials' salaries and yet allot, as we have done, forty million pounds for productive projects? What would have happened if we had opened the coffers of the treasury of the state, as they had done, and distributed their contents among officials and let come what may thereafter. The year that ensued would have found the Government unable to pay the salaries of officials.

How easy it would have been to satisfy all those malcontents! But what is the price that our country would pay out of its hopes and its future for that satisfaction?

PART III

PART III

In Part I, I discussed how the revolution first started within us as individuals, in ourselves as normal types of the youth of our generation. I spoke of the revolution and its place in the history of our people, and of July 23rd as a day in that revolution. In Part II, I dealt with the attempts we made as we proceeded along the road to revolution and how our national history has determined that road, whether in our consideration of the past, a consideration full of morals, or in our aspiration of the future, an aspiration charged with hope.

On those previous occasions I spoke of "time" but the "place" also claims its right. Let me therefore speak of "place" on this occasion.

I do not aim at a complicated philosophical discussion of "time and place" but there is no doubt that the world and not our country only is the result of the reaction of time and place. In depicting the circumstances of our country, I said we could not forget the element of "time." We cannot forget the element of "place" either.

In simple language, we cannot go back to the

Tenth Century and wear its robes which strike us as being curious and ridiculous now-a-days. Neither can we lose our way in the ideas which appear in front of us utterly black without a single ray of light filtering through them. In the same way we cannot act as if our country is a part of Alaska in the Far North or as if we are on Wake Island which lies distant and deserted in the vastness of the Pacific.

We should first of all agree upon one thing before we proceed further and that is to define the boundaries of place as far as we are concerned. If I were told that our place is the capital we live in I beg to differ. If I were told that our place is limited by the political boundaries of our country I also do not agree. If our problem, as a whole, is confined within our capital or inside our political boundaries, it will be easy. We would lock ourselves, close all the doors and live in an ivory tower away as much as possible from the world, its complications, its wars and crises.

But the era of isolation is now gone. Gone are also the days when barbed wires marked the frontiers separating and isolating countries, and every country must look beyond its frontiers to find out where the currents that affected it spring, how it should live with others . . . etc. It has become imperative that every country should look around itself to find out its position and its environment and decide what it can do, what its vital sphere is and where the scene of its activity and what its positive role could be in this troubled world.

As I often sit in my study and think quietly of this subject I ask myself, "What is our positive role in this troubled world and where is the scene, in which we can play that role?"

I survey our conditions and find out we are in a group of circles which should be the theatre of our activity and in which we try to move as much as we can.

Fate does not play jokes. Events are not produced haphazardly. Existence cannot come out of nothing.

We cannot look stupidly at a map of the world not realizing our place therein and the role determined to us by that place. Neither can we ignore that there is an Arab circle surrounding us and that this circle is as much a part of us as we are a part of it, that our history has been mixed with it and that its interests are linked with ours. These are actual facts and not mere words.

Can we ignore that there is a continent of Africa in which fate has placed us and which is destined today to witness a terrible struggle on its future? This struggle will affect us whether we want or not.

Can we ignore that there is a Muslim world with which we are tied by bonds which are not only forged by religious faith but also tightened by the facts of history? I said once that fate plays no jokes. It is not in vain that our country lies to the Southwest of Asia close to the Arab world, whose life is intermingled with ours. It is not in vain that our country lies in the Northeast of Africa, a position from which it gives upon the dark continent wherein rages today the most violent struggle between the white colonizers and black natives for the possession of its inexhaustible resources. It is not in vain that Islamic civilization and Islamic heritage, which the Mongols ravaged in their conquest of the old Islamic Capitals, retreated and sought refuge in Egypt where they found shelter and safety as a result of the counterattack with which Egypt repelled the invasion of these Tartars at Ein Galout.

All these are fundamental facts, whose roots lie deeply in our life; whatever we do, we cannot forget them or run away from them.

I see no reason why, as I sit alone in my study with my thoughts wandering away, I should recall, at this stage of my thinking, a well-known story by the Italian poet Luigi Pirandelli which he called, "Six Personalities in Search of Actors."[1]

The annals of history are full of heroes who carved for themselves great and heroic roles and played them on momentous occasions on the stage. History is also charged with great heroic roles which do not find actors to play them on the stage. I do not know why I always imagine that in this region in which we live there is a role wandering aimlessly about seeking an actor to play it. I do not know why this role, tired of roaming about in this vast region which extends to every place around us, should at last settle down, weary and worn out, on our frontiers beckoning us to move, to dress up for it and to perform it since there is nobody else who can do so.

Here I hasten to point out that this role is

[1]"Six Characters in Search of An Author," by Pirandello, is apparently here meant.

not a leading role. It is one of interplay of reactions and experiments with all these factors aiming at exploding this terrific energy latent in every sphere around us and at the creation, in this region, of a tremendous power capable of lifting this region up and making it play its positive role in the construction of the future of humanity.

There is no doubt that the Arab circle is the most important and the most closely connected with us. Its history merges with ours. We have suffered the same hardships, lived the same crises and when we fell prostrate under the spikes of the horses of conquerors they lay with us.

Religion also fused this circle with us. The centres of religious enlightenment radiated from Mecca, from Koufa and later from Cairo.

These were also collected in an environment in which all these historic, spiritual and material factors are closely knitted. As far as I am concerned I remember that the first elements of Arab consciousness began to filter into my mind as a student in secondary schools, wherefrom I went out with my fellow schoolboys on strike on December 2nd of every year as a protest against the Balfour Declaration whereby England gave the Jews a national home usurped unjustly from its legal owners.

When I asked myself at that time why I left my school enthusiastically and why I was angry for this land which I never saw I could not find an answer except the echoes of sentiment. Later a form of comprehension of this subject began when I was a cadet in the Military College studying the Palestine campaigns in particular and the history and conditions of this region in general which rendered it, throughout the last century, an easy prey ravaged by the claws of a pack of hungry beasts.

My comprehension began to be clearer as the foundation of its facts stood out when I began to study, as a student in the Staff College, the Palestine campaign and the problems of the Mediterranean in greater detail.

And when the Palestine crisis loomed on the horizon I was firmly convinced that the fighting in Palestine was not fighting on foreign territory. Nor was it inspired by sentiment. It was a duty imposed by self-defense.

I do not want now to discuss the details of the Palestine War. This is a subject that needs several many-sided discussions. But one strange lesson of the Palestine War I care to mention:

The Arab nations entered the Palestine War with the same degree of enthusiasm. They all shared the same feelings and had known quite well the limits of their security. They came out of the war with the same bitterness and frustration. Everyone of them was thus exposed, in its own country, to the same factors and was governed by the same forces, that caused their defeat and made them bow their heads low with shame and humiliation.

I sat by myself several times in the trenches and dug-outs of Iraq-el-Manshia. I was then the staff-officer of the sixth company, which held this sector, defended it sometimes and used it for attack often.

I used to walk amidst the ruins all around me, which were left after the bombardments of the enemy. There I travelled far in my imagination. My voyage took me to the sphere of the stars where I would regard the whole area from my great height above.

From the height of the stars above I used to come down to earth often and feel that I really defended my home and my children. Neither my dreams, the capitals, the states, the people, nor history meant anything to me then. This was how I felt when, in my wanderings I came upon the

children of refugees who were caught in the ten-
tacles of the siege after their homes had been
demolished and their property lost. I particularly
remember a young girl of the same age as my
daughter. I saw her rushing out, amidst danger
and stray bullets and, bitten by the pangs of
hunger and cold, looking for a crust of bread or
a rag of cloth. I always said to myself, "This
may happen to my daughter." I believe that
what was happening in Palestine could happen,
and may still happen today, in any part of this
region, as long as it resigns itself to the factors
and the forces which dominate now.

After the siege and the battles in Palestine I
came home with the whole region in my mind
one complete whole. The events that followed
confirmed this belief in me. As I pursued the
developments of the situation I found nothing
but echoes responding one to the other. An event
may happen in Cairo today; it is repeated in
Damascus, Beirut, Amman or any other place
tomorrow. This was naturally in conformity
with the picture that experience has left within
me: One region, the same factors and circumstances, even the same forces opposing them all.
It was clear that imperialism was the most prominent of these forces; even Israel itself was but

one of the outcomes of imperialism. If it had not fallen under British mandate, Zionism could not have found the necessary support to realize the idea of a national home in Palestine. That idea would have remained a foolish vision, practically hopeless.

As I put down these impressions, I have before me the memoirs of Chaim Weizmann, the President of the Republic of Israel and its real founder. These memoirs were published in his famous book called "Trial and Error." They contain certain passages worthy of consideration on account of the particular stamp they bear.

I pause at the following: "It was essential," Weizmann wrote, "that a big power should assist us. There were two great powers in the world who could give us this assistance: Germany and Britain.

"As for Germany it preferred to keep away and avoid any intervention. Britain was sympathetic and patronizing."

Again I pause as I behold Weizmann saying:

"It happened during the Sixth Zionist Conference which we held in Switzerland that Hertzel stood declaring that Great Britain only, of all the states of the world, has recognized the

Jews as a nation in an independent form and apart from others.

"We, the Jews," he continued, "are worthy of having a home and being a state."

Hertzel then read a letter to that effect from Lord Latterson on behalf of the British Government. "In this letter," he said, "Lord Latterson offered us the territory of Uganda to be a National Home. The members of the Conference accepted the offer. After that we suppressed and checkmated this proposal at its early stage and buried it without clamour. Britain again sought to satisfy us. After this proposal we formed a commission of a considerable number of Jewish savants, who proceeded to Cairo to study the territory of Sinai. There they met Lord Cromer, who sympathized with our aspiration to achieve a national home. Later, I met Lord Balfour, the British Foreign Secretary, who hastened to ask me, 'Why didn't you accept Uganda as a National Home?'

"I replied, that Zionism is a national and political movement is true but there is also the spiritual side which we cannot overlook. I am certain that if we ignore this spiritual aspect we shall not be able to realize our political and national vision. I also asked Balfour, 'What would you

British Information Services

Lord Balfour, author of the
Balfour Declaration

Wide World

Chaim Weizmann, founder of
State of Israel

United Nations

Mahmoud Fawzi, Foreign Minister, United Arab Republic

do if somebody would suggest you take Paris instead of London? Would you accept'?"

I also ponder over another passage in Weizmann:

"In the Autumn of 1921 I returned to London where I was called to supervise the drafting
of the covenant of the British Mandate in Palestine. The rough draft should have been submitted
to the League of Nations in order that it might
adopt a resolution upon it. Afterwards the Conference of St. Remo approved the very idea of
the Mandate.

"Lord Curzon had then replaced Lord Balfour as foreign secretary and was responsible for
the drafting of the covenant. With us in London
then was the great jurist, Ben Cohen, one of the
ablest authors of legal formulae in the world.
Eric Adam, Curzon's secretary, also cooperated
with us. We had a difference with Curzon, a difference which was the first and last.

"We had recorded in the draft of the covenant
a clause pledging Britain to the Balfour Declaration, and demanding that its policy in Palestine
should be on the basis of a National Home of the
Jews. The text of the clause we wrote was as
follows: 'And the recognition of the historic
rights of the Jews in Palestine.' Curzon proposed

that this clause should be toned down so as not to arouse the Arabs when they read it. He proposed it should read: 'And the recognition of the connections of the Jews and their historic relations with Palestine'."

I wish to continue quoting from Weizmann's "Trial and Error," but we know that these old incidents were the first germs of the dreadful repercussions that tore Palestine into shreds and destroyed its very existence.

I now revert to what I was discussing, namely, that imperialism is the great force that throws around the whole region a fatal siege.

I thus began to believe after these facts became established within me, in one common struggle and repeated to myself, "As long as the region is one, and its conditions, its problems and its future, and even the enemy are the same, however different are the masks that the enemy covers its face with, why should we dissipate our efforts?" The experience of what followed July 23rd increased my faith in a united struggle [to unify the Arab regions] and its necessity.

I confess I also began to visualize the great obstacles that blocked the way of a united struggle. But I also believe that these stumbling blocks should be removed because they are the work of the one and the same enemy. The primary obstacle in our path is "suspicion." The seeds of that suspicion were sown in us by the common enemy in order to stand between us and the united struggle.

I do not hesitate for one moment to mention that our united struggle would achieve for us and our peoples everything we wish and aspire to; I shall always go on saying that we are strong but the great catastrophe is that we do not know the extent of our strength.

We make a mistake in our definition of power. Power is not merely shouting aloud. Power is to act positively with all the components of power.

When I attempt to analyze the components of our power I cannot help but point out three principal forces of power which should be the first to be taken into account.

The first source is that we are a group of neighboring peoples joined together with such spiritual and material bonds as can ever join any group of peoples. Our peoples have traits, components and civilization, in whose atmosphere the three sacred and heavenly creeds have originated. This cannot be altogether ignored in any effort at reconstructing a stable world in which peace prevails.

As for the second source it is our territory itself and the position it has on the map of the world, that important strategic situation which can be rightly considered the meeting-place, the cross-road and the military corridor of the world.

The third source is petroleum which is the vital nerve of civilization, without which all its means cannot possibly exist whether huge works for production, modes of communication by land, sea and air, weapons of war whether they are planes flying above the clouds or submarines submerged under layers of water. All these, without petroleum would become mere pieces of iron, rusty, motionless and lifeless.

I wish I could linger a while and discuss petroleum. Its existence, as a material fact established by statistics and figures, is worth making it a model for a discussion of the importance of the sources of power in our countries.

I have read lately a treatise published by The University of Chicago on the state of petroleum. I wish every individual of our people could read it, ponder upon its meanings and give free play to his mind to realize the great significance which lies behind figures and statistics. This treatise shows for example that to extract the petrol of

72

Arab countries would not cost a great deal of money.

Petrol companies have spent 60 million dollars in Colombia since 1916 and have not found a drop of oil until 1936. These companies also spent 44 million dollars in Venezuela and did not find a drop of oil until after 15 years.

These companies again spent 30 million dollars in the Dutch East Indies and have not struck oil until very recently.

The final conclusion of this treatise is as follows:

The capital necessary for extracting one barrel of petrol in the Arab countries is ten cents. The centre of oil production has shifted from the U. S. A., where oil wells have been exhausted, where the price of land is exorbitant, and where wages of workers are high, to the Arab territory, where the wells are untouched and in a virgin state, where expensive land can be had for nothing and where labour accepts subsistence wages.

It is a fact that half the world's reserve of petroleum is still underground in the Arab regions and the second half is distributed among the U. S. A., Russia, The Caribbean and other countries of the world.

It is also established that the average output of one well of oil per day is as follows:

11 Barrels in U. S. A.

230 Barrels in Venezuela

4,000 Barrels in the Arab Region

I hope I have succeeded in explaining clearly the degree of importance of this element of power.

We can consider ourselves, therefore, powerful, though not in the loudness of our voices whether we cry, wail, or appeal for help, but powerful when we sit calm and count in figures our capacity for work, powerful in our thorough understanding of the strength of this bond which links us and which makes our territory one.

Such is the first circle in which we must revolve and attempt to move in as much as we possibly can. It is the Arab circle.

If we direct our attention after that to the second circle, the circle of the continent of Africa, I would say, without exaggeration, that we cannot, in any way, stand aside, even if we wish to, away from the sanguinary and dreadful struggle now raging in the heart of Africa between five million whites and two hundred million Africans.

We cannot do so for one principal and clear reason, namely that we are in Africa. The people

Nasser delivers deed of land ownership to Egyptian peasant

Oil in the Middle East

of Africa will continue to look up to us, who guard the northern gate of the continent and who are its connecting link with the world outside. We cannot, under any condition, relinquish our responsibility in helping, in every way possible, in diffusing the light and civilization into the farthest parts of that virgin jungle.

There is another important reason. The Nile is the artery of life of our country. It draws its supply of water from the heart of the continent.

There remains the Sudan, our beloved brother, whose boundaries extend deeply into Africa and which is a neighbour to all the sensitive spots in the centre of the continent.

It is a certain fact that Africa at present is the scene of an exciting ebullition. White man, who represents several European countries, is trying again to repartition the continent. We cannot stand aside in face of what is taking place in Africa on the assumption that it does not concern or effect us.

The third circle now remains; the circle that goes beyond continents and oceans and to which I referred, as the circle of our brethren in faith who turn with us, whatever part of the world they are in, towards the same Kibla in Mecca and

76

whose pious lips whisper reverently the same prayers.

My faith in the positive efficacy which can be the outcome of further strengthening the Islamic bonds with all other Muslims became deeper when I went to the Saudi Kingdom with the Egyptian mission who went there to offer condolences on the occasion of its late King.

As I stood in front of the Kaaba and felt my sentiments wandering with every part of the world where Islam had extended I found myself exclaiming, "Our idea of the pilgrimage should change. Going to the Kaaba should never be a passport to heaven, after a lengthy life. Neither should it be a simple effort to buy indulgences after an eventful life. The pilgrimage should be a great political power. The press of the world should resort to and follow its news; not as a series of rituals and traditions which are done to amuse and entertain readers, but as a regular political congress wherein the leaders of Muslim states, their public men, their pioneers in every field of knowledge, their writers, their leading industrialists, merchants and youth draw up in this universal Islamic Parliament the main lines of policy for their countries and their cooperation together until they meet again. They should meet reverently, strong, free from greed but active, submissive to the Lord, but powerful against their difficulties and their enemies, dreaming of a new life, firm believers that they have a place under the sun which they should occupy for life."

I recall I expressed some of these sentiments to His Majesty King Saoud. He said to me, "This is the real wisdom of the pilgrimage." Verily I cannot visualize a higher wisdom.

When my mind traveled to the eighty million Muslims in Indonesia, the fifty in China and the several other million in Malaya, Siam and Burma and the hundred million in Pakistan, the hundred million or more in the Middle East and the forty in Russia as well as the other millions in the distant parts of the world, when I visualize these millions united in one faith I have a great consciousness of the tremendous potentialities that cooperation amongst them all can achieve: a cooperation that does not deprive them of their loyalty to their countries but which guarantees for them and their brethren a limitless power.

I now revert to the wandering role that seeks an actor to perform it. Such is the role, such are its features and such is its stage.

We, and only we, are impelled by our environment and are capable of performing this role.

APPENDIX

BIOGRAPHICAL NOTE
NASSER AND NEGUIB

By John Gunther[1]

Lieutenant Colonel Gamal Abdel Nasser (correctly Gamel Abd Al Nasir) was born on January 5, 1918, and is of modest bourgeois background. His father was a post-office clerk in Alexandria; his mother was the daughter of a businessman. From the age of seventeen Nasser had strong revolutionary tendencies. He was several times arrested for participation in student riots. He went to the Renaissance Secondary School in Cairo, studied law for a time, and then decided to devote himself to the army. He was commissioned in 1938, served for a time in the Sudan, and fought against the Jews in Israel. But even while campaigning in Palestine he records that he was fully aware that the "real" battleground would be Egypt itself. One turning point of his life came in February, 1942, when, as mentioned above, the British unleashed tanks and machine guns against Farouk's palace. Nas-

[1]From "Inside Africa" by permission of Harper and Brothers. The name Neguib has two acceptable spellings: Neguib or Naguib. Gunther's use of the second has here been changed for consistency with both Badeau's and Nasser's usage.

ser had no particular use for Farouk, even in those days, but he was the King, and that he should be humiliated and browbeaten so flagrantly seemed to Nasser an intolerable affront to Egyptian dignity. What an irony it is that it should have been the same Nasser who, ten years later, destooled the profligate King and hurled him out of the country!

Nasser is a tall, large, gracefully built man with remarkable eyes and a big rudder of a nose. His personal habits are exemplary. He lives with complete lack of ostentation in a modest Caïro villa, and his personal life has been happy. He has five youthful children.[2] He is a devout Muslim, and does not touch alcohol. He has acute interest in politics all over the world, and is one of the few African — or European — statesmen who subscribe to such periodicals as *Foreign Affairs* not by ordinary post but by airmail. The dominating aspect of his character is disinterestedness plus force. He cares nothing for himself; all that interests him is the life of Egypt. He is much more reserved and less turbulent than most Egyptians, and his businesslike clarity of

[2]In 1934, Nasser married Tahia Mohamed Kazem, an attractive woman who is a talented pianist. She never accompanies her husband to the President's official residency, the Koubbeh Palace but remains with their children in the suburban army barracks which is their simple private home. — *Editor's Note.*

manner shows little of the inferiority-superiority sensitiveness and lack of poise that distinguish many of his compatriots.

This is not to say that he has ever lacked emotion. I heard him described as a man of ice — and fire. He took part during the war in an attempt to force the release of the deposed prime minister, Aly Maher, from detention; he looked for guidance for a time to such extremists as Hadj Amin El Husseini, the exiled Grand Mufti of Jerusalem; he was an early member of the Muslim Brotherhood, and on one occasion even flirted with the idea of assassinating the King.

What is more, Nasser took active part in another murder plot which, however, miscarried. He has described this himself, in a series of three articles for the Egyptian magazine *Akher Saa,* entitled "The Philosophy of the Egyptian Revolution," which he wrote in 1953.[3] Few documents of our time are more revealing. It is a rare thing, to put it mildly, for a man who is running a country to confess that only a few years before he had been leader of a murder squad. He does not reveal the name of the intended victim, but describes in considerable detail his own emotions.

[3] I have had access to a privately circulated translation of these. They were printed in part in the London *Observer,* October 10, 17, and 24, 1954.

At this time he and his fellows were convinced that nothing but "positive action," that is political assassination, could save Egypt . . .

Nasser's articles are of absorbing interest, showing as they do the convulsion of agony that gripped his mind, and also how half-baked some of his thinking was. Ceaselessly he reflected on the weakness of his country, its degradation and shame. Egypt had to be redeemed; it had to be saved not merely from the British[4] but from itself; it had to be made strong, united, free, with a new cleanliness of spirit, with corruption and selfishness abolished. But how?

Nasser took the lead at last in organizing the Free Officers Committee, composed of some four hundred youthful men, most of them under the rank of major. In effect, it is still this body that rules Egypt today . . .

Nine officers composed Nasser's original Revolutionary Council, which grew out of the original Free Officers Committee. Neguib was not among them, but was brought into it because the clique needed an older man, a soldier with authority and prestige, to give it respectability. Nasser plotted the coup, and then sold it to Neguib. The junta, under Nasser's guidance, moved in

[4]Nasser uses the locution "the Imperialism" as a synonym for "British."

the early hours of July 23 with force and pre-
cision. Tanks commanded strategic points in
Cairo, and radio broadcasts announced to the
nation that the army had moved "to purify itself." There was no bloodshed or disorder. There
were no demonstrations against foreigners—if
only because Nasser did not want to give the
British any pretext for stepping in. An incidental point is that the plotters maintained close
contact with the American embassy as soon as the
coup got underway, and got strong sympathy
from Americans in Cairo . . .

Nasser-Neguib borrowed ideas from Fascism,
but they were much less totalitarian and extremist
than those who opposed them. Their methods
may have been totalitarian, but not the basic aim.
Membership in the new Liberation Rally was
voluntary, not obligatory. There was no accent
on force for force's sake. Almost at once every
effort was made to work out a system of consti-
tutional reform, and pave the way for free elections and the resumption of democratic government. The army was the protector of the people,
and the revolution was in the people's name . . .

One persistent, almost ineradicable source of
dissidence and turmoil was the Muslim Brotherhood. This, a body which combined extreme na-

85

tionalist aims with a kind of fundamentalist religious fanaticism, was not so much a party as a movement. It grew up after World War II, and had several million members at the height of its power. It wanted freedom from Britain above all, believed in political terrorism, and assassinated two Egyptian prime ministers and other folk. At one time Nasser, as I have already mentioned, belonged to this organization, and so probably did several other members of the cabinet and the Council of Revolutionary Command. Also it was penetrated strongly by Communists. Nasser-Neguib tried to cooperate with the Brotherhood at first. A certain identity of purpose linked them, particularly in religious matters. But they were bound to come into conflict, if only because there was not room in Egypt for two revolutionary mass movements. The Brotherhood began to make agitation against the government, and in January, 1954, it was suppressed; 450 of its leaders were arrested, two thousand local headquarters were shut down, and $8,500,-000 of its funds were confiscated. But it refused to stay suppressed. Its supreme "guide," Hassan El Hodeiby, was released from jail after a time and trouble began anew. In October came an attempt by members of the Brotherhood to assassinate Nasser; eight shots were fired against him, but he escaped untouched. This time the government moved against the Brotherhood in real earnest, and it was crushed and broken up to such an extent that it is doubtful if it can ever rise again. Six members implicated in the murder plot against Nasser were hanged, and so was its secretary general, Abdel Kader Auda. El Hodeiby, an old friend of Nasser's, was "sent in irons to Toura prison to break stones for the rest of his life."[5]

The October episode also served to end General Neguib as a political force. He was removed from office (November, 1954) and placed under arrest. Probably he had nothing to do with the plot against Nasser, but Brotherhood terrorists said that they planned to make a new revolutionary government under his (Neguib's) leadership. Whether or not the General was aware of this conspiracy to make use of him is unknown.

The breakup of the Nasser-Neguib relationship is one of the saddest of contemporary political episodes. Neguib had great quality and brought much to the revolution. The two men complemented each other nicely. Nasser was the brain, the theoretician, the organizer; Neguib was

[5]*World Today*, February, 1955.

87

the doughty and incorruptible man of action, wildly popular with the masses. For a time there was a profound fondness between the two partners as well as close political affiliation. What, in the end, caused the split? First, pressures within the army. Second, Neguib wanted a quick return to a normal parliamentary regime, but Nasser thought that the people were not yet ready. Neguib is much more moderate than Nasser, much less inclined to push through a truly revolutionary program on a long-range basis. Third, temperamental differences growing into acute bitterness and jealousy ...

Nasser first emerged into public view when he became deputy prime minister and minister of the interior on July 18, 1953. Before that, very few people indeed outside the inner circle even knew his name. Seldom has any country experienced a more sinuous merry-go-round than what followed. We must foreshorten the story drastically. Conflict between the two men became open, Nasser was the stronger, and on February 25, 1954, Neguib was forced to resign from all his major posts. Nasser became prime minister and chairman of the Council of Revolutionary Command. But the announcement of this change-about produced such a fierce storm in Cairo that it had to be revoked; also intense pressure from the Sudan, where Neguib was universally regarded as a savior and a hero, forced Nasser to reconsider. Nasser, having got rid of the front man, found that he was so popular that he had to be taken back. So after three days of commotion Neguib reassumed the presidency, but not the premiership. But almost immediately — on March 8 — came another development, caused by a crisis over votes within the junta itself. A compromise was worked out whereby Neguib lost control of the Council of Revolutionary Command, but became prime minister again. On March 27 - 29 a further complex evolution came, with such attendant tension that a state of emergency had to be declared in Cairo. Neguib remained nominally president and premier, but his power disappeared. Then on April 17, for the second time within two months, Nasser (who had become deputy prime minister) replaced him as prime minister. Finally came the November explosion over the Muslim Brotherhood, and Neguib passed entirely from the scene. Nasser took over the chairmanship of the Council of Revolutionary Command and the duties of head of state, though the actual office of president was left vacant . . .

To return to Nasser. What he needs most, as is only too obvious, are time and political tranquility. He cannot get the former without the latter. To rule successfully he must hold the good will of the people at large, and not let his government degenerate into a purely military junta, exercising authority capriciously. But to rule at all he has to hold the reins firm, and this he cannot do — for the time being at least — without maintaining arbitrary rule.

One thing can be said without question — already he has done more for Egypt in a couple of years than the royal family did in a hundred and fifty. He is absolutely honest and has never asked anything for himself. The very fact that he is both dedicated and honest is a phenomenon so puzzling to old-style Egyptians that they cannot "understand" him. I heard him described as a "simple man with a complex mind." But, after all, that is better than being a complex man with a simple mind.

WHAT IS NASSER LIKE?

By Richard D. Robinson[1]

Now that United Nations Secretary General Dag Hammarskjold has returned from his Middle East mission, we ask ourselves again, What are Nasser's objectives?

Many Americans believe that President Gamal Abdel Nasser of Egypt, who came to power in 1954, is just another tin-horn dictator and self-seeking opportunist. Others contend that he strives toward constructive ends with which the West should be identified.

Motivation and goals are difficult to judge, even in face-to-face contact with individuals of one's own nation. We can go only by the record. In so doing, we must assume a man innocent of evil intent until proved guilty.

In the case of Nasser, evil cannot be equated simply with anti-Western or neutralist thought and action. What we must prove is that he is acting contrary to the interests and welfare of the

[1]Lecturer at Harvard University; staff member of Harvard Center for Middle Eastern Studies. Taken by permission from Foreign Policy Bulletin, October 15, 1958, Foreign Policy Association, Inc.

Arab peoples. And in making such a judgment we must measure existing regimes, not against an ideal that may not be attainable, but against possible alternatives — in the case of Egypt probably either a Communist take-over or the recurrence of religious fanaticism.

President Nasser is one of the first of the modern Arab leaders to face up in a realistic way to such problems as land reform, industrial development, honesty in government, mass education, and so on. It is too early to judge results, but programs of social and economic development are Nasser's stock in trade. A large part of his popularity in the Middle East is due primarily to his closer identification with genuine social and economic reform than is true of other contemporary Arab leaders.

Virtually every Western student of Middle Eastern affairs agrees that the prime prerequisites for really significant economic development of the Arab states are some kind of regional union and an honest, reform-minded government. About half of the population of the Arab Middle East — that of Egypt — is now confined to 35,168 square kilometers in the Nile Valley, with virtually no oil. And much of the wealth in the balance of the Middle East is concentrated in a few hands.

Given the mutual jealousy and the tenacity with which the various competing monarchs, sheiks and other petty Arab politicians protect their privileged positions, it is unrealistic to expect the achievement of Arab unity within the foreseeable future without some violence. Many of these Arab leaders have shown callous disregard for the welfare of their own peoples until hustled into belated and half-hearted reform through fear of either Nasserism or Communism, or both. Actually the record shows that, as great revolutions go, Nasser-led Arab nationalism has been remarkably free of violence. And Nasser himself has repeatedly expressed personal repugnance for violence, which he regards as self-defeating in many situations.

An obvious precondition for instituting regional unity and honest reform government is a generally recognized, forceful leader. Nasser comes the closest to filling this role.

Under these circumstances, Western moves to keep the Arabs divided among and against themselves have in fact blocked the general development of the area. So also have any Western moves to shore up disliked, opportunistic and

corrupt regimes — often created in the first instance by the Western powers. Not even the
Western press can make such regimes, now under attack, locally popular.

Nasser's Record

Many American editorial writers and others
charge that Nasser's "positive neutrality" is
nothing but a sham, just another word for destructive nationalism and political opportunism.
It is true that in any mass movement there are
destructive elements. But let us look at the other
side of the record.

The Suez Canal has been kept open by the
Egyptians and not used for political blackmail,
as many had feared at the time of nationalization.
The Egyptians on July 13 accepted a mutually
satisfactory agreement with foreign stockholders
on compensation for the canal — yet many West-
erners had said that this could never take place.
And little known to the American public is the
fact that, after nationalization, Nasser invited a
group of American business interests to operate
the canal.

None of the Nasser-oriented states — Egypt,
Syria, Iraq — tolerate a domestic Communist
movement. None of these states have stopped

the flow of oil to the West. And it was only Syria's union with Egypt under the protective mantle of the United Arab Republic (UAR) which halted Syria's drift into the Soviet orbit. On several occasions Nasser applied to the West first for military and economic assistance, and in every instance he took precautions to avoid direct Soviet intervention in the Middle East. So far Nasser gives no indication of being a Soviet tool or of being directly responsible for revolution in Iraq or unrest in Lebanon.

The mere evidence that the Lebanese rebels received some UAR assistance does not transform Lebanese unrest from civil war into aggression. So far no evidence of massive UAR aid to the Lebanese rebels has been presented, according to the United Nations Observation Group.

One further point should be borne in mind. It is misleading to measure the Egyptian regime by the yardstick of Western democracy. The adoption of democracy in Egypt now would merely condemn the country to the return of a corrupt, self-serving, Farouk-like regime. Today the social, educational and economic level of Egypt is not adequate to support a democracy. Just as Kemal Atatürk's dictatorship (1923-1938) prepared Turkey for a limited form of democracy, so perhaps Nasser's authoritarian regime will prepare Egypt for eventual democratization. But much has to be done before that time arrives. It took Turkey 26 years to modernize its society, and even today democracy is still seriously challenged there — not by self-seeking politicians but by the still considerable weakness of the economic, educational and social systems. For democracy requires at least a minimum of popular enlightenment and some economic strength.

It would be well for Americans to withhold judgment until all the evidence is in — and that may be some years away. Is Nasser another Atatürk, or isn't he? No one now knows, for power can corrupt. But it need not — as witness Atatürk. In passing final judgment we must bear in mind that Atatürk had two advantages over Nasser — an economically viable country and a relatively homogenous people. And, strange to recall, in the early days of the Atatürk revolution, Turkey's only external assistance came from the Soviet Union.

ARAB NATIONALISM AND NASSER

By George Kirk[1]

Arab nationalism is as old as Islam itself. In Islam God finally revealed Himself to men through the Arabic language, and the Arab's speedy conquest of a great empire seemed the outward sign of divine favor. In later centuries this sense of being a chosen people had to be shared with the whole supranational community of Islam, and so it remained until modern times. Almost all the Muslim Arabs within the Ottoman Empire regarded that empire as continuing to typify the divinely ordained supremacy of Islam.

The Young Turk revolution of 1908 awakened hopes of reform, but instead of fulfilling these hopes, the Young Turks sought to impose a narrowly Turkish nationalism throughout the empire. Consequently some Muslim Arabs were thrown into association with Arabic-speaking Christians who had been acquiring the Western

[1]Professor Kirk, a lecturer at Harvard University's Center for Middle Eastern Studies, has been a student of the Arab world since 1935. Taken by permission from Foreign Policy Bulletin, November 15, 1958, Foreign Policy Association, Inc.

19th-century concept of secular nationalism. Modern Arab nationalism is the offspring of this marriage of ideas.

The nationalists, however, were still a small minority. Their limited contribution to the overthrow of the Ottoman Empire in World War I did not, in the eyes of the world statesmen who made the peace in 1919, give their political ambitions an automatic priority over the ambitions of Britain, France and the Zionists in the Middle East for which historic justification was also claimed. During the subsequent 30 years of struggle the Arab nationalists, using both diplomacy and force, gained ground, but they still remained short of their goal.

By 1946 seven Arab states — Egypt, Iraq, Syria, Lebanon, Saudi Arabia, Jordan and Yeman — had achieved independence and had formed a loose association in the Arab League. This, however, was far from satisfying the intellectuals' desire for Arab unity. In 1947 the Palestine issue afforded an occasion for demonstrating that unity in action. At that time the Arab governments and peoples resolved to defy the United Nations and forcibly prevent the establishment of the state of Israel. In this undertaking they failed. Although official apologists sought excuses in the undoubted partiality toward Israel shown by the UN majority and in the destructive rivalries between Arab governments, the more honest Arab critics were left with the bitter conviction of failure both in leadership and self-discipline.

The reforms attempted in Egypt by Neguib and Nasser after the military coup of 1952 that ousted King Farouk evoked the spontaneous approval of nationalists in the neighboring Arab countries. But although Egypt had from the outset played the leading role in the Arab League, an Egyptian nationalism focused on the Nile Valley was of longer standing and of more immediate appeal to most Egyptians than the wider nationalism of the Arab League. During their first two years in power Egypt's young and inexperienced military rulers concentrated their efforts on immediate problems in Egypt and the Sudan. Their main concern outside seemed to insure that no Arab state should diverge from Egypt in its foreign policy.

By the end of 1954 Gamal Abdel Nasser had become the unrivaled leader of the new Egypt. His book, *Egypt's Liberation: The Philosophy of the Revolution,* suggests that he might, in any case, have aspired to a wider Arab leadership once the British had agreed to terminate their hold on the Suez Canal. As events turned out, however, challenges which the Egyptian military regime encountered in the winter of 1954-55, on both domestic and international fronts, caused it to repair its shaken prestige by recourse to the emotional appeal of pan-Arab nationalism. The action which finally assured the nationalists' support of Nasser was his 1955 arms deal with the U.S.S.R. At last Arab nationalism had found a great power which, it thought, would help it to achieve independence and unity. In the Arab's view Britain had "betrayed" the Arabs after World War I; Nazi Germany had encouraged Arab extremists in World War II and had then failed them. By contrast, the U.S.S.R. had an obvious interest in extruding the hostile West from the Middle East.

Nasser's Prestige Triumphs

Since 1955 Nasser's policy has won him a series of prestige triumphs, especially with the middle-class youth of the Arab cities. To more experienced observers, however, it has also demonstrated Egypt's military weakness when tested, as well as its economic isolation and financial poverty amid the rising pressures imposed by its rapid population growth. The regime has been forced to put off its long-term schemes of economic and social improvement and to substitute short-term "shots" of nationalist prestige. The establishment of the United Arab Republic is the latest of these prestige injections, although the hangover phase of this cycle is already evident. The revolutionary schism of the Arab world between conservative and radical factions — a cleavage which coincides to some extent with the division between the older and younger age groups, as well as between privileged and non-privileged — has been sharpened by the fact that the radicals, after many disappointments, have found their "charismatic leader." Meanwhile, however, the originally opportunist and maneuverable Egyptian dictatorship seems to be becoming the prisoner of doctrinaire ideologies.

For the radical idealists of Arab countries, Arab political unity is, or should be, a natural consequence of the linguistic and cultural affinity of the Arab world, and any religious or social minorities — notably in Lebanon — which resist speedy unification are to be brought into line by subversion or force. These radicals, moreover, are probably ready to grasp the proferred aid of the U.S.S.R. — notably for financing the High Aswan Dam — more trustingly than is Nasser himself. Nasser is thus faced with the dilemma of either allowing himself to be swept by the popular tide of revolutionary nationalism into dangers — both intra-Arab and international — which in his moments of reflection he would rather bypass; or of putting on the brakes and thereby risking the alienation of the revolutionary elements who are his ardent vocal supporters now, but — as happened in Palestine in 1948 and in Sinai in 1956 — would prove useless in a major crisis.

Nasser may still have some margin of choice left, but time is short. Meanwhile, the best-intentioned offers of Western cooperation for the economic development of the Middle East seem either premature or, at best, palliatives.